D1276773

# Words For Elephant Man

# Words For Elephant Man

Kenneth
Sherman

*Etchings*
George
Rabb

◥◣ MOSAIC PRESS

## Canadian Cataloguing in Publication Data

Sherman, Kenneth, 1950–
  Words for elephant man

Poems.
ISBN 0-88962-200-0 (bound). – ISBN 0-88962-199-3 (pbk.)

I. Title.

PS8587.H483W67      C811'.54      C83-098407-0
PR9199.3.S5W67

Published by Mosaic Press, P.O. Box 1032, Oakville, Ontario L6J 5E9, Canada.

Published with the assistance of the Canada Council and the Ontario Arts Council.

Typeset by Speed River Graphics.
Design by Doug Frank.
Printed and bound by Les Editions Marquis Ltée, Montmagny, Québec.
Printed and bound in Canada.

ISBN 0-88962-200-0 cloth
ISBN 0-88962-199-3 paper

Distributed in the United States by Flatiron Books, 175 Fifth Avenue, Suite 814, New York, N.Y. 10010, U.S.A.

Distributed in the U.K. by John Calder (Publishers) Ltd., 18 Brewer Street, London, W1R 4AS, England.

Distributed in New Zealand and Australia by Pilgrims South Press, P.O. Box 5101, Dunedin, New Zealand.

For Irving Layton

# CONTENTS

A PSALM OF THE ELEPHANT MAN                                    11

I *SHOWMAN*                                                    15

MYSTIQUE                                                       17
THE SHOW                                                       18
A DEAD ELEPHANT                                                19
LIVING CONDITIONS: WINTER, 1884                                20
FREAKS                                                         21
THE ONLY ELECTRIC LADY                                         22
FIRST MEETING TREVES                                           23
BEFORE THE PATHOLOGICAL SOCIETY OF LONDON                      24

II *ORIGINS*                                                   27

THE CAUSE                                                      29
WOMBWELL'S ROYAL MENAGERIE                                     30
THIS CITY                                                      31
THE WRONG ONE DIED                                             32
THE SKY OVER LEICESTER NEVER GOT THAT COLOUR                   33
THE CURE                                                       34
THE CONGREGATION                                               35
IN THE YEAR OF OUR LORD, 1875                                  36
ONE MOTHER                                                     37
INTO THE WORKHOUSE                                             38
DECEMBER 25, 1880                                              39
OUT                                                            40
THE WRITER                                                     41

III *DISLOCATIONS*                                             45

THE SHOW, IN ENGLAND, IS CLOSED                                47
AQUARIUM                                                       48
ARRIVAL BACK IN LONDON: POLICEMAN'S REPORT                     50
TREVES' DESCRIPTION OF MERRICK                                 51
NURSES                                                         55
BEDSTEAD SQUARE                                                56
TWO FANTASIES                                                  57
ROMANCE                                                        59
A PRETTY LADY                                                  60
ELEMENTAL                                                      61

I FEED THE HUNGERING MULTITUDES              62
VICTORIA           63
EVERYTHING          64
THE WORD          65
A VISIT TO THE THEATRE          66
CORRECTION: A VISIT TO THE ZOOLOGICAL GARDENS,
LONDON          67
THE MODEL CHURCH          68
TO THE COUNTRY          69
TREE          71
THE ANIMAL SIDE          72
IN THE COUNTRY          73
NOWHERE          74
INCURABLE          75
GOING OUT          77
A DISPLAY IN THE LONDON HOSPITAL MUSEUM          79
FROM THE *DESCRIPTION OF THE SKELETON OF "THE* 81
*ELEPHANT MAN" IN THE CATALOGUE OF THE MUSEUM OF*
*THE LONDON HOSPITAL MEDICAL COLLEGE*

# Words For Elephant Man

# A PSALM OF THE ELEPHANT MAN

What protrudes from my upper jaw
what makes of my mouth a shattered clam
a tortured vent.

My speech is indistinct,
                    my vowels rise
like wild birds,
                    my consonants grind
and splutter
            like an engine's damaged
gears,
        my peculiar limp
                        beats time.

This is the song of thy suffering servant.
This is the articulation of the New Age.
This is God's hobbling little poem.

I drone on in His image.

I

# SHOWMAN

*It was not the show,
it was the tale that you told.*

# Mystique

There is a picture
painted on canvas
that hangs before this shop:

ELEPHANT MAN
               TWO PENCE

and the creature
not half and half
but more of the man
than the beast
in the process of
changing.

The colours are
olive green, white,
and blood red,
a thick garish fantasy
while in the background —
palm trees, coconuts.

Of course it has to be
in a foreign land,
it has to be
exotic.

Each night
               I dream
herds of white elephants

thundering
               across a rural
English green.

# THE SHOW

Tom lifts the canvas.

Robed in white
               like a degenerate Roman senator

I stand some minutes
with my back to them
letting their eyes

               grow wide

                    swim out in circles

over the countours of my head.

                   I own them
and let the tension grow
               to the right moment

then turn
        and drop the robe.

They push
        en masse
               long neck of some straining beast:

shouts of disgust
           shrieks
               some laughs.

In another stall
a limbless boy from India
eats glass while standing
on his head,
          says
in his land
elephant man is Ganesh,
god of wisdom.

# A DEAD ELEPHANT

*I had mistimed my tour, still in Newcastle-upon-Tyne with less than two weeks till the opening of Bartholomew Fair. The possibility of my reaching London in time with my procession of caged beasts looked remote in the extreme. It was at this point I got wind of the fact that my arch-rival, Atkins, was promoting his menagerie at Bartholomew as "the only wild beast show in the fair". Without hesitation I undertook an epic forced march, bringing my caravanserai to London the day the fair opened. But the effort took its toll on my elephant. The poor beast dropped dead on arrival. Atkins lost not a moment in claiming he had "the only living elephant in the fair" at which I counterattacked with the slogan "The only dead elephant in the fair". The tactic paid off, since a dead elephant was a greater rarity than a live one and my show was crowded every day of the fair while Atkins's was comparatively deserted.*

—George Wombwell

# LIVING CONDITIONS: WINTER, 1884

Fireflies about the gas lamp
about the heated brick
                    (my furnace)

small light
            to pick the lice
hidden in my weathered robe.

My breath
            is a ghost fragment
sifting over hands.

Day after day
                the customers' eyes
cut like glass through my silence

to where my flesh
                burns winter white.

Do you know what it means

                        to be a legend in your time

to sleep
        in a straw filled stall?

# FREAKS

Across the road
in Whitechapel
they exhibit the women
Jack the Ripper did in.
In wax, of course. A drained
white, the stab wounds
running like scarlet buttons
and laces from each neck
down to the pubic hair.

The Alligator Boy
in the stall beside me
jokes, calls it
Jacque's Place. A showman
bags pennies, unwinds
the terrors

       the crowd:
black silk hats
white scarves
women's parasols

women.

At night
      they are murdered.

In the light of day
        they are sold.

# THE ONLY ELECTRIC LADY

As a young man, Tom Norman paid a penny
to see *The Only Electric Lady:*
                          sparks
flew like inchworms of light
                          from her body.
When he touched her hand
                          the shock of it
bolted him back.

Later, he discovered she was connected
(as was the metal plate under the damp
carpet on which the customer stood)

to an electric coil.
                  *It was,*
Tom said,
          *like seeing the soiled underpants of God.*

For his first show, *Savage Zulus,* he
hired unemployed seamen,
                          painted them black.

*It was not the show,*
                  he used to say,
*it was the tale that you told,*

though with me he never had to say a word.

I was beyond metaphor,
                  my stench
cutting through the intricacies of fiction.

That is why when Treves came to see me
they had to fetch Tom in a pub,

                                        he
was drinking,

                  he was dreaming

*The Only Electric Lady.*

# First Meeting Treves

Treves arranged for my
visit here: they
photograph me,
measure my head, my limbs,
take a blood sampling.
I try talking and my voice
like a caged bird suddenly let loose
bounces off the lab white walls.
Treves writes on his chart
*imbecile*, when really
it's men speaking two
different languages:

he, the words of a man who has everything

me, the words of a man who has words

# BEFORE THE PATHOLOGICAL SOCIETY OF LONDON

*longitudinal sulci*
*subcutaneous tissue*
*papillomatous growth*

That too is language
                      designed to keep you
five steps away,
                explain my pain.

In this medical theatre
                    minds are thumbing back
through a thousand yellowing texts:
mouths move
           as by rote

(a row of ventriloquists' puppets)

while their eyes,
                human and horrified,
                          flash
like frantic lanterns
                  through the caverns of
my flesh.

        *What is it?*
        *What is it?*

Gentlemen,
            do you not know revelation
when you see it,
                my figure
                        naked and hunched

a curdled question mark
                  that breathes?

# II

# ORIGINS

*I supposed that Merrick was imbecile and had been imbecile from birth. The fact that his face was incapable of expression, that his speech was a mere spluttering gave grounds for this belief. The conviction was no doubt encouraged by the hope that his intellect was the blank I imagined it to be. That he could appreciate his position was unthinkable.*

Sir Frederick Treves

# THE CAUSE

the expectant mother should

    keep herself cheerful
    listen to good music
    frequent art galleries

she must not

    hide a leaf in her bosom
    eat strawberries
    allow fruit of any sort to fall on her
    (all of the above resulting in a baby
    with birthmarks)

she must not
have liver thrown in her direction
(in that case the child will have freckles)

try to avoid the sight of the chimney sweep
in case the baby be born
black skinned

above all,
avoid connections of any sort with
unfamiliar
animals

# WOMBWELL'S ROYAL MENAGERIE

Outside:                painted panels of lush
impossible jungle

barechested men wrestling ferocious
lions

the serpent, fork-tongued, thick
as a tree

Inside:                  parched fairground

tethered camels

shedding lamas

lions leaping dutifully
through hoops

then there were the elephants
larger than any canvas,
                        they loomed above the
citizens of Leicester
                my home town
                                where my mother
herself crippled, pregnant,
                        went to watch the slow
parade of those great grey beasts
                                linked tail
to tail.

        She stumbled
                        and fell,
                                their monster columns
brushing against her,
                        their trumpeting cries
reverberating
            through her womb.

# T HIS CITY

where once a year

        the River Soar

                floods

raw sewage, garbage

our Venice of turds and gnawed ribs

oil and steam

this black and white city
churned by finance

this slummed madness

this wet rat's head

this peeling paint
of rooms the size of cupboards

where infants
        give out

go soft as spoiled fruit.

# THE WRONG ONE DIED

My younger brother William and I
had scarlet fever.
He died, age 5.
I survived.

He was smooth of limb,
he would have been
handsome.

I lie in bed.
I peer into the dark
listening
to my mother's sobs
now and then
her high
piercing laughter.

Hour by hour
I feel my body swell.

Soon
I shall fill completely
the nothingness
that surrounds me.

# THE SKY OVER LEICESTER NEVER GOT THAT COLOUR

These women
bone close
to the terror of nature.

Take mother for example:
first I come along
teaching her
what hideous things
can thrive inside a womb.

Then little William
wasted by scarlet fever —
her burnt angel
age five.

She became a Baptist
school teacher.
As I grew uglier
and uglier
she grew more and more
religious

over her bed
a portrait of Jesus

his flesh
unblemished

his eyes
a magical
crystal blue

# THE CURE

which isn't.
        At five the tumours first appeared.
Mother took me to see a woman in Leicester's lower end.
She wore a white shawl, a black dress, her hair
hung in grey greasy strands,
                    her forehead furrowed
as if she was struggling against the whine of those engines
that never ceased, not for a godly moment

                                  she seemed to be
squinting through a millenium of wet steam


                she advised:

                        leeches
                        bleeding
                        hot cups

none of which helped.

                It was as if God had planted
some terrible thing in me that kept blossoming and
blossoming

        at first firm, like rooted bulbs,

then dangling
            like dead and reeking flowers.

At age 20
I entered the Royal Infirmary
where a Dr. Marriott
                cut 4 ounces of flesh
                          from my upper lip.

# THE CONGREGATION

I sit alone
        in the back row

my elaborate head

            weighing
                on the dark wood

of the bench before me.

                Crimson, some
silver,
      a smell of camphor,
            the light
like dull brass

        poured through leaded windows.

One by one

      their heads

           turn from the vacant cross

to catch a glimpse

        of this body.

# IN THE YEAR OF OUR LORD, 1875

Father got me a licence to hawk:
gloves, stockings, general haber-
dashery. Mother worked hours
sewing clothes to fit
                          and still
I was a sight.
                    A small crowd
always followed me
                          some bought
from pity
              some for the novelty

while some went on
                          witty
at my expense.

                    Man is a
fascinating animal,
                    I have had
the opportunity to study him
from many different angles,

                                    once
I passed a mirror in a hat shop
window and stared at myself
and the people jeering about me.

I stared and stared and then I
cried,
            not just for me,
                                    but for
the spectacle,
              the story.

# ONE MOTHER

Mother died when I was eleven
and my world fell through.
                              Six months later
father married a thin-lipped widow with three
normal brats
                    their favourite pastime
aping me.


                    So often at dinnertime
I would find myself hungry,
                              huddled
in the doorway of a closed and darkened shop,
my rough cheeks stained with tears.

There were some lines mother found for me
when I was still a child.
                              They went like this:


    *'Tis true my form is something odd*
    *But blaming me is blaming God.*
    *Could I create myself anew*
    *I would not fail in pleasing you.*


But on those evenings
in those dark doorways
other lines came back to me,
lines
from one of her hymns:


    *God gives each of us only one mother*
    *And after her death, there is no other.*

# INTO THE WORKHOUSE

the drunk, the old,
those poor   through injury
             through lunacy

the young unwed women
who are pregnant —

runs in the new social fabric
the tireless, shining engines weave.

Then there is me.
             A doctor once remarked
had I not had this affliction
I would have been good looking.

Behind the bulging bone, the bales
of skin,
        can you see
me?

   My left arm has gone untouched.
It is the one visible part of which I am proud.
As the rest grows thicker and thicker,
                          it seems
thinner, a child's limb,
                a branch
off the tree in Eden.

                When the bell rings
I put down my mallet
                and limp
into the dining hall where even the most
ravenous put down their spoons

        raise disbelieving eyes.

# DECEMBER 25, 1880

It is Christmas in the workhouse.
All of London is still.
A fine drizzle falls.

You can smell the dinner
they are preparing for us:
pork, plum pudding — a heavenly
break from our daily bowl of "hell-broth".

Even the more manic lie in their beds
silent, contemplating the grey light
that sifts down from high, murky windows.

I have kept count:
over the past six months I have unravelled
hemp amounting to 1500 pounds, tearing
strands thin as hair from old ropes,
my hands blistering maggot white.

Would that make enough for a new rope
I could wrap about the equator,
I wonder what they'll do if my hand
gets much thicker,
           my body
a breathing tuber
only to be watered?

In the cobblestone courtyard
men in navy blue uniforms,
eye-stained, reeking of gin,
stand guard over our tree,

silvered and glittering.

# O<small>UT</small>

Is there a way out
>           of these 4 walls

my heart
>       hammered,
>>              a stone's white powder,

my ears charged
>>          with the mallet's
monotonous rhyme.

>>>              Today, two of our guards
showed me an advertisement
for Tom Norman's novelty show,
nudging each other,
>>              smirking,
>>>                  suggested
I'd make a fine display.
>>>          I played
their game,
>>          hunched, sang hymns, recited
naughty ballads
>>>          while they slapped their guts
and laughed

>>              (It got me out of work
for a full 45 minutes
>>>              I asked

if I might borrow the advertisement

>       and one of the guards

crumpled it into a ball

indicating my distorted hand

>>>              said *Catch*

# THE WRITER

Dear Mister Tom Norman,

It has come to my attention that you are this country's leading showman. Well Sir, as mother used to say, God helps those...

My head is 36 inches round
with a substance of flesh
at the back
large as a breakfast cup.
The other part is like hills
and valleys
all lumped together.

My right hand is the size and shape
of an Elephant's fore-leg,
the other, no larger than
that of a girl of ten.

My face is such a sight
that none could describe it
in fact one would not believe,
until they saw it,
that such a thing could exist

(do I have your interest?)

Mother also talked of hell fire. She, however, had never been inside a workhouse where I have dwelt these past four years.

You Sir, could be a saviour

J. Merrick

or

The Elephant Man?

41

# III

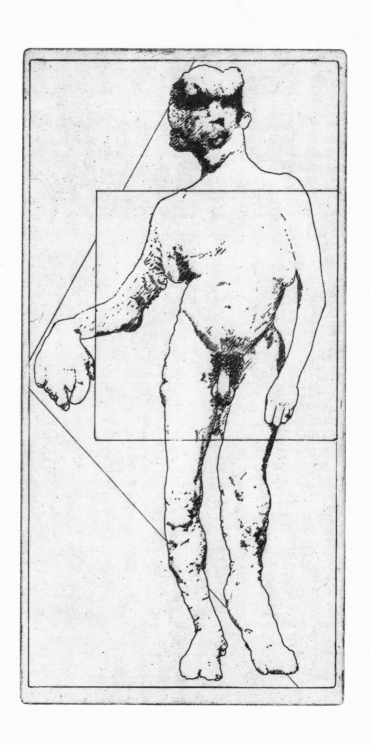

# DISLOCATIONS

*In order apparently to bring the meter still more within the sphere of prose and common speech, Hipponax ended his iambics with a spondee or a trochee instead of an iambus, doing thus the utmost violence to the rhythmical structure. These deformed and mutilated verses were called lame or limping iambics. They communicated a curious crustiness to the style. The choliambi are in poetry what the dwarf or cripple is in human nature. Here again, by their acceptance of this halting meter, the Greeks displayed their acute aesthetic sense of propriety, recognizing the harmony which subsists between crabbed verses and the distorted subjects with which they dealt — the vices and perversions of humanity — as well as their agreement with the snarling spirit of the satirist. Deformed verse was suited to deformed morality.*

John Addington Symonds, *Studies of the Greek Poets*, Vol. I, 1873

# THE SHOW, IN ENGLAND, IS CLOSED

Because they flocked to see me
street urchins, peddlers, prostitutes,
general labourers —
the sort I lived amongst in Leicester's lower end —
as well as the respectable
blushing against their black capes

Because they'd pay for a viewing
in every hamlet from Nottingham
                                        to London

Because I was the real thing
no phony cannibal, no midget
posing as the deposed King of Siam

Because my flesh went beyond
the words on my pamphlet
the crude painting on my advertisement

the age's
            Doppelganger

        its underside

        its Hyde

# AQUARIUM

I was sent to the continent where my manager, an Austrian,
abandoned me in Brussels, took my life savings of 50 pounds.
That night I huddled in the doorway of a bakery,
watching the rain fall like mercury pellets

my loneliness
                    churning to fear.

Morning, the slick cobblestones, dank odour of worms.
Out of the early fog
as out of a hazed nightmare
I see myself
                    a squat shape
                    in black cap, black coat
                    phantom veil with slits for eyes
                    limping
                    on a twisted stick.

The market's first farmers pointed, their urgent
foreign tones pushing me on to Ostend
where the captain of the Dover ferry
gingerly lifted my veil,
                    grimaced,
refused me passage.

              I stood on the deck's wet wood
raw smell of gulls and fish,
my heart
        plunging through the chill grey water
my tongue
           moored in my mouth.

I sobbed
till someone stepped forward,
led me to a carriage
paid my fare to Antwerp.

Against the windows
the waiting passengers pressed
their palms
          their faces

flat white undersides
             of sea creatures.

# ARRIVAL BACK IN LONDON: POLICEMAN'S REPORT

*At 5 a.m., during my patrol of Liverpool Street Station, I noticed, amidst the unusually large morning crowd, said subject, face veiled, standing on platform by gate number 7. He had just disembarked, carried no luggage, turned about several times apparently not knowing which way to proceed.*

*After not too long a time a crowd had gathered about said subject. As is usual with crowds, it soon grew rapidly in numbers. At this point I spotted constables Pierce and Wiggins entering the station and approached them. Together we attempted to dispel the crowd, and only just managed in leading said subject into the third-class waiting room where constables Pierce and Wiggins held the doors of the waiting room against the press of persons who clamoured to be let in.*

*Said subject collapsed into the furthest and darkest corner of the room. I approached, the veil was lifted, and here I must admit my recollection is marred for it took some time for me to overcome my shock at the sight of said subject's features. Whether it was this surprise or the high-pitched run-together speech of said subject I am not sure, but I could not distinguish any meaning to what was being said. The subject did eventually produce from an interior pocket a small oblong of much-thumbed pasteboard which read:*

> Frederick Treves
>
> General Surgeon
>
> London Hospital

*I henceforth dispatched a boy to summon said Treves.*

# TREVES' DESCRIPTION OF MERRICK
(Included is the latter's gloss)

> He (Merrick) had learned to read and had
> become a most voracious reader. The Bible
> and Prayer Book he knew intimately.
> —Sir Frederick Treves

*The most striking feature about him was his*
*enormous and misshapened head. From the brow*
*there projected a huge bony mass like a loaf,*
*while from the back of the head hung a bag of*
*spongy, fungous-looking skin, the surface of*
*which was comparable to brown cauliflower.*

> All who see me mock at me,
> they make mouths at me, they wag
> their heads.

*On top of the skull were a few long lank*
*hairs. The osseous growth on the forehead*
*almost occluded one eye.*

> What the eye sees the mind reads,
> what the mind reads ...
> I hobble down darkened alleys,
> behind me
>            the clatter of tin cans.

*From the upper jaw there projected another*
*mass of bone. It protruded from the mouth*
*like a pink stump, turning the upper lip*
*inside out and making of the mouth a mere*
*slobbering aperture.*

> I search    in the refuse of East End
>             in the song of the Queenly Prostitute
>             in the Rubber Man's dignified death
>
>             a new language

*The nose was merely a lump of flesh,*
*only recognizable as a nose from its position.*

That which is there and called that
because it is always there and
always called that.

*The face was no more capable of*
*expression than a block of gnarled*
*wood.*

What they nail me to.

*The right arm was of enormous size*
*and shapeless. The hand was large and*
*clumsy — a fin or paddle rather than*
*a hand.*

Will you put Leviathan on a leash
for your maidens
Will traders bargain over him
Will they divide him up among merchants

*The thumb had the appearance of a*
*radish, while the fingers might have*
*been thick, tuberous roots.*

God's own morsel.

*The other arm was remarkable by contrast.*
*It was not only normal but was,moreover,*
*a delicately shaped limb covered with fine*
*skin and provided with a beautiful hand*
*which any woman might have envied.*

I am sick with love.

*From the chest hung a bag of the same*
*repulsive flesh. It was like the dewlap*
*suspended from the neck of a lizard.*

My heart is like wax,
it melteth within my breast.

*The lower limbs had the characters of*
*the deformed arm. They were unwieldy,*
*dropsical looking and grossly misshapen.*

I am poured out like water
and all my bones are out of joint.

# Nurses

The first one who saw me
dropped her tray and fled.
After that, I am sure it became a challenge —
compassion's final chalice.

                    The faces
of the younger ones are nondescript
liked puffed up pillows. They mostly
hold their breaths
and turn the other way.

                    The older ones,
gaunt-faced, owl-eyed
from having seen
all there is to see
(so they thought)
                    turn
when I catch them staring.

                    Lately
I have been wondering
what stories they tell
when they return to their homes

whether they have become famous
on their respective streets
for having touched my sacred flesh.

# BEDSTEAD SQUARE

*...because here the iron beds*
*were marshalled for cleaning and painting.*

At night I am permitted to walk.

I pick my way through rusted frames,
through bolts and mildewed mattresses:
the bones and bowels of beds in repair.

                    Here
they need many many beds.

Further on
         the square is checkered
by the light from high windows.

                    I inch,
a damaged pawn,
           beyond the end
of East Wing
         to where the hospital gardens lie:

lush grass,
         thick redolence of night flowers.

Sometimes, if the sky is clear, I am
very careful and tilt my gallon head
to glimpse the splattering of stars,
                the moon
a mute white imprint
           on the endless dark.

The garden
        and the hospital:

              *rust and petals*

              *rust and petals*

# TWO FANTASIES

## I

I dream of those asylums
where the poor blind are kept.
Perhaps I may be permitted to live there
among the gas-lamps and shadows
among those who move with halting steps.

One day a door will open
and a woman in a white night dress,
long black hair

a face both young and sad,
somehow aged and therefore
so beautiful

shall enter and edge
across the room

run her hand
over my face,
my limbs,

reading with
tenderness

these lines
of pain.

## II

My other fantasy is to live alone
in a lighthouse,
                    like the one I saw
in a picture of Eddystone.

I will be the light
bringing fishermen home to their families.

I will be the other moon
that opens
in the viscous dark

a white wound
brighter than polished tusks.

I will be the watchful eye
of the Lord of gross tumours
perched
atop this lonesome column of stone

welcoming you by night
into a world I cannot enter

spend my days
dreaming about.

# ROMANCE

Everything was marred, distorted,
except my left arm and my love apparatus.
                                        Here
is Treves the scientist:

> *The genitalia remain normal and untouched*
> *among all the deformities.*

Here is Treves, the man of memoirs:

> *He would like to have been a lover,*
> *to have walked with the beloved object*
> *in the languorous shades of some*
> *beautiful garden,*
> *and to have poured into her ear*
> *all the glowing utterances*
> *that he had rehearsed*
> *in his heart.*

# A PRETTY LADY

*It became a cult among the personal friends
of the Princess to visit the Elephant Man.*

Treves brought her in, it was a coolish spring day.
She smiled, she wore a mauve dress, I could
hear the hem of it as she crossed the room,
it was the sound of water.

I was wood. I was part of my chair. When she
took my hand and said "So happy to make
your acquaintance"

            I cried.

                 I cried and cried and cried.

Some men want the world. I only want to be
lovable.
       Am I lovable? Is there a shudder
of eros
       in all this wattled ugliness?

The countesses, the actresses, the Princess Alexandra:

I have all their photographs,
               signed,
                   smiling at me
from atop my dark commode.

               After we have chatted,
exchanged pleasantries, views on literature,

          they leave
          (they always leave).

I claw the air
       where their perfume
             lingers.

# ELEMENTAL

In Leicester's lower end
they crucified me.

Here
they dress me in tweeds
           collars
           ties.

What does my brown bulbous hand
have to do with the starched white cuff
it juts from?

Am I decorous enough
do I fit your image
of sweet savage
suited, saved
speaking your
tea sipping language

my flesh
tendrils of thankfulness

twisting and twining
about your
polished heart?

# I FEED THE HUNGERING MULTITUDES

Last week
        to help the hospital
                raise money for my keep,

the Master of the Temple
            preached a sermon
                      on the question:

"Who did sin,
          this man or his parents,
                   that he was born blind?"

Two days later
          the *London Times* ran a special —

photographs, interviews:

          Here I am, trying on a
hand knitted sweater from one of the hospital's donors.

          Here I am, sitting in a chair
now known as *CHAIR OF THE ELEPHANT MAN.*

Everything I touch
          turns to future gold.

Years down the road,
          the auctions:

        *ELEPHANT MAN'S NAIL CLIPPERS*

        *ELEPHANT MAN'S LOVE LETTERS*

        *one of ELEPHANT MAN'S EXCISED TUMOURS*
(preserved in formaldehyde)

# VICTORIA

Perhaps what fascinates them most
is the story I use
                    to explain
                              the origin
of my condition,

                    how my mother
was frightened by an elephant.

At night, I imagine a man
                              returned from his visit here.
He puts aside
              his cape
                    and silver-headed cane

his black
        hat

              undoes the starched collar

lies down to sleep

                    and dreams a tremendous
                                        trunk

groping
        through a drawer
                    of silken bloomers.

# EVERYTHING

Treves asks what I wish for Christmas.

I show him an advertisement for a dressing bag.

(a) I cannot use the silver-backed brushes
    because my hair has fallen out.

(b) The ivory handled razors are useless
    because I cannot shave my face.

(c) The deformity of my mouth
    renders the toothbrush unusable.

(d) The cigarette case, ditto, since my monstrous lips
    could never hold a cigarette.

(e) The silver shoe horn could not help
    with my ungainly slippers.

(f) The hat brush is unsuited
    to my peaked yachting cap.

In short, the gift is useless.

Treves believes I want it because I like to think of myself as
(these are *his* words):

> *the Piccadilly exquisite*
> *a real swell*
> *a dandy*
> *a Don Juan*
> *a gallant*
> *the young spark*

What in fact had attracted me

        was the caption over the ad:

**\*FOR THE GENTLEMAN WHO HAS EVERYTHING\***

# THE WORD

One day you will know
it was not neuro-fibro-
matosis,
      nor any of your other
damned specimens of language.

Rather, it was the word
I could not sing.

      Once I tried
and someone taped a pound note to my lips;
I tore it off and the monstrous hiss of
the engines drowned me out.

What's the use, I thought, watching
men leave whole each morning,
return in the dark like small change.

So I held in the word
but the consonants
      battered against my palate,
fell back, flattened and dull as worked metal.

Those few vowels that escaped
were thin wind
      down a stinking mineshaft.

The word tried new exits,
      blasting bone,
pushing out these pendulous folds

till I became the abc of pain

till I became the sound
      skewered through flesh

straining
      with the terror of an epic.

# A VISIT TO THE THEATRE

I sit with Treves
                    in the shadow

of the Baroness' box.

                              Before my eyes,
          a pantomime,
                    a fairy tale
                              entitled *Puss & Boots*:

poor penniless boy meets magical cat,

cat introduces boy to princess,

cat takes boy to ogre's castle

turns ogre into mouse,

eats same,

gives boy castle,

boy can now marry princess.

A fantasy?
A Victorian morality play
(this great age of empire, politics and helpers
helpers helpers)?

I, the poor boy.
Treves, the cat.

Where is the princess?

# CORRECTION: A VISIT TO THE ZOOLOGICAL GARDENS, LONDON

There is the elephant, eyes closed,
God's dreaming boulder
                        lost in meditation
                                    upon his former lives.

His wide hide
            caked and cracked
by sun of savannahs
                is forgiving as mud

his ears
        are harmless rays
                    undulating in an ocean of air

his trunk
        a blind gigantic tuber,

                            the snout
pink hibiscus.

What have I in common with his calm,
his ease with straw and defecation,
                            his slack
perpetual grin?

Look at the cat pacing that cage,
his anxiousness —
                    something to do with
the finality of stone,
                    black bars,
                                that
and the gawking well-dressed crowds.

Even at rest his contempt is clear,
                            his eyes
the underworld's fire and dark,

                        compressed
cooled and solidified
                    into two smooth stones

glaring with the certainty
                of the final word.

# THE MODEL CHURCH

My bad arm dangles by my side —
a shattered log —
                   while with the good one
I piece together this model.

Have you noticed the detail,
                   the perfectly
rendered spires and gables, the intricate
roof pattern, the weathervane, the carefully
placed windows?

I leave it to posterity; let it serve to perplex:

God created a creature whose ugliness
made men wince — a model of imperfection
who fed on poetry, who moulded such
architectural beauty

(only man thinks in the perfect
                   tense).

Lately, I dream more and more of visiting the country.

I've grown sick of this city's strict greys

               whites and blacks:
                       its churches
                       and courts

                       its brothels
                       and slums

I long to see a gnarled tree with red blossoms

               weeds that bloom blue

# TO THE COUNTRY

When I arrived, the maid, having not been properly informed of my (what shall I term it, state? condition?) of my appearance, dropped her tray (once again the sound of shattered glass) and fled. She told the carriage man she could not care for me as she was in danger of being permanently "all of a tremble". I was conveyed then to a gamekeeper's cottage, hidden from view, close to the margin of a wood (once again I live on the edge).

This gamekeeper is used to wonders of nature. He and his wife break bread with me and afterwards, sing hymns. There are some dried pelts on the wall and an engraving of a street fair in London, the city to which their son has moved and which they have no wish to visit.

# TREE

I have sat in this forest for hours
contemplating colours.
They vanish
like paint
on porous rock.

Always,
      my mind locks back
with the horrid fixity of a photograph
into black and white —
               limited

                             but what I know.

In this photo, for instance, my two arms:
the one I call good because it looks
like other arms
and the one I call bad,

the one that is different.

I have lived my life
stretched between them

asking what it would take to
go beyond
           to become the gnarled singing tree
upon which
           no forbidden fruit is grown

nor any man hanged.

# THE ANIMAL SIDE

I stumble down paths
my leathery limbs
smashing through branches,
                              leaves.

What if a hunter should come upon
me, take me for the animal side
and shoot?
                    What would he make
of the volume I clutch in my hand,
the portrait of a woman
                              in the locket
dangling from my neck?

Would he think I am mutant

something stepped out of a myth

would it matter to him?

I must move carefully

I must try to make sounds
that are human

                    (in dreams
                              I have seen my head

bony and grey
                    mounted on a wall

                    miraculously

                              singing)

# IN THE COUNTRY

The day is too hot
the sun
zeroing in,
a scalpel to the eyes.

*Too bright,*
            I slouch
from darker dreams:

                        factories
                        side-shows

                        caves
                        subterranean alleys

before that
the cold and murky deep
where cells in fury split —
nature's mindless multiplication
into spore and tree.

The problem here
is that I see,
            in ponds
in rivers
            my halved image

the problem here is that
I interpret
            the flies

that sing
            about my temporary flesh.

# NOWHERE

It is evening.
The eyes of animals peer out
from the forest,
shiny and wet.

Too exotic for even their world
I sit on a black rock
which took wind and earth
aeons to create.

I am closer to the moss, to the
fungus
            or perhaps to that flower
blown colourless
by today's storm

its stem bent,
it seems to be held  up
by its crutches of thick leaves.

On the road back to the cottage
my moonlit shadow
                        limps ahead.

I will never catch
up with it,

it looks
like the figure
of another man.

# INCURABLE

I have returned
        to my underground apartment.

Day and night
        I cannot help
                but hear the groans
of those above,
        those who strive,
                those for whom there is
a cure.

        In vases,
                the flowers I brought back
from the country,
                static and dry.

                        They are
what they are
        and aspire to nothing more,

their shadows
        stippling the late afternoon wall.

So beautiful,
        they flicker
                like will-o'-the-wisps

as darkness
        seeps through these rooms.

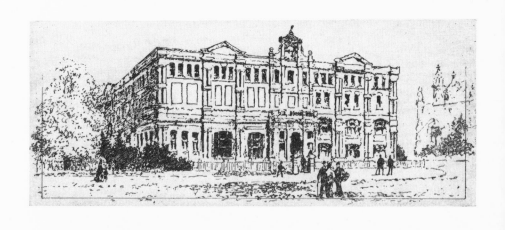

# GOING OUT

*The attitude he was compelled to assume when he slept was very strange.
He sat up in bed with his back supported by pillows, his knees drawn up,
his arms clasped round his legs, while his head rested on the points of his
bent knees.*

*He often said to me he wished he could lie down to sleep "like other
people". I think on this last night he must, with some determination, have
made the experiment.*

Tonight
        I am smooth
                as gelatin

clear as ice
        tall
            and handsome.

Tonight
        my silken tongue
                is courtesy of

Tennyson,
        my heart,
            a love song by Sullivan

swept away
        with fays,
            princes

at last
      part of
          the audience.

Lie down
        sleep
            and dream

       *        *        *        *        *

Sinking
        through fathoms of cool and vacant dark

pinpricks of white,
          the memory of shattered glass

or the residue of a now forgotten alphabet

             suspended like stars

till I am
      as I was

          before age 5
          before the candle wax began

          my fair head, bonnetted,
                my body
        soft consonant,
            a garden of promises

(where do they store all the tears that have been shed

and what is that meagre globe of light
up ahead,

     a planet,

       something created,

or a way out,

     a man's last O

        scalding the dark?)

# A DISPLAY IN THE LONDON HOSPITAL MUSEUM

Now you have it all:
> the cap
and veil,
> the cloak, the
slippers like big paper bags

my bones.

The man you talked with
for hours,
the one who sobbed uncontrollably
when a lady took his hand,
the one who
quoted Caliban and built
the model church

you dissected.

What did you find?

When the bones were put
together was whatever
you were looking for

there?

Did you hear
what Lady Kendall referred to
as my *voice so strangely musical*

echoing
> in the dark

against the glass
> of the display case

the cold
> bronze plaque?

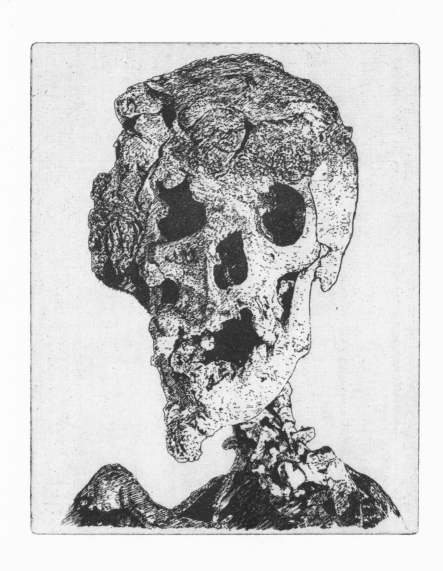

# F ROM THE
*DESCRIPTION OF THE SKELETON OF "THE*
*ELEPHANT MAN" IN THE CATALOGUE OF THE MUSEUM*
*OF THE LONDON HOSPITAL MEDICAL COLLEGE*

## GENERALIZED HYPEROSTOSIS WITH PACHYDERMIA

*...The bones of the right carpus are large and friable*
*the phalanges and metacarpals*
*of the index*
*right and little fingers*
*are of large size and soft texture.*
*The bone of the thumb present*
*normal characters.*

| *Upper Limbs:* Comparative weights (dry) | *Right.* | *Left.* |
|---|---|---|
| Clavicle | 3 ¹/₈ oz. | 1¼ oz. |
| Scapula | 3 | 1¾ |
| Humerus | 6 | 4 |
| Ulna | 4¼ | 1¼ |
| Radius | ¾ | ½ |

Factual information about the Elephant Man came from Ashley Montagu's *The Elephant Man: A Study In Human Dignity* (E.P. Dutton, 1979) and *The True History Of The Elephant Man* by Michael Howell and Peter Ford (Penguin Books, 1980). Both books contain Sir Frederick Treves' classic essay "The Elephant Man" from *The Elephant Man And Other Reminiscences* (Cassell & Co. Ltd., 1923).

A number of the poems and prints were previously published in *Descant*.

## ABOUT THE AUTHOR

Words For Elephant Man is Kenneth Sherman's third book of poetry. His previous books are Snake Music (Mosaic Press, 1978), a collection of poems partly based on his travels in Asia, and The Cost Of Living (Mosaic, 1981) which Quill & Quire called "... an impressive collection ... shows Sherman's power and promise."

Kenneth Sherman lives in Toronto with his wife and daughter and teaches in the General Studies Department at Sheridan College.

# ABOUT THE ARTIST

George Raab was born in Marseilles, France in 1948. He studied at the University of Toronto, later creative arts (specializing in printmaking) at Sheridan College in Oakville, and etching at Erindale College in Streetsville, Ontario. He has travelled extensively in Africa, Europe, the Middle East, and the Canadian arctic.

Principal collections include the Art Gallery of Ontario, the Toronto Dominion Bank, the Canadian Imperial Bank of Commerce, the University of Toronto, Clarkson Gordon Canada Ltd., Art Gallery of Hamilton and the Canada Council Art Bank, as well as private collections throughout Europe and North America.

His numerous awards include, most recently, the Print and Drawing Council of Canada's G.A. Reid Memorial Fund Award at the Second Canadian Biennial of Prints and Drawings and the top prize for prints at the Prestigious American Biennial of Graphic Arts held at the Museo de Arte Moderno La Tertulia in Cali, Columbia, South America.

He has held many one-man exhibitions as well as participating in group shows in both Canada and the United States. His work is represented by galleries in major Canadian and American cities.